Praise for
LIVE for JOY

"One of this decade's philosophers ... Anne Scottlin's words of wisdom come like raindrops on dry land."
—Mohammed Darweesh, Madrid

"Anne Scottlin is a thought leader of scope and depth, a role model of impact."
—Anthony C. Gruppo, CEO, Author/Speaker, New York

"Anne shares her voice of wisdom in a time when so many people need that comfort and guidance. Her well-chosen words hold more power than ever before."
—Julie Parker, San Francisco

"In Anne's words I find hope and encouragement to defy the odds."
—Johnny Chase, North Carolina

"I've been waiting for someone with Anne's ability to motivate and give me confidence. Her quotes have inspired me to take action in my life in areas where I was holding back."
—Jonathan Marsh, UK

"Anne's inspiration carries a tremendous message of empowerment."
—Albert N. Rundu, Namibia

"True words for people, companies and countries." —Yves Morier, Deutschland

"I always eagerly anticipate Anne's work. Her words bring hope, promise and sunlight to an often dark world."
—Gary Canning, UK

"Anne is an exceptional and inspirational leader."
—Fred Westrip, California

"Anne's words bring so much needed positivity, reminding me that the sun still shines even in the darkest storm."
—Esoche R., Washington D. C.

"Anne's quotes always spread love, kindness and inspiration."
—Meela S., Newcastle, South Africa

More Content By Anne Scottlin
#ScottlinTalks / Scottlin TV
For schedules and content see www.annescottlin.com
Twitter @AnneScottlin

For information about special discounts for bulk purchases or author interviews, appearances and speaking engagements please contact:

The Power of Joy
Scottlin International
+1 323 741 2814
contact@annescottlin.com

First Edition

Compiled, designed, produced by Rodney Miles
Original book and cover design by Will Caminada
Image Selection by Anne Scottlin

LIVE for JOY

Anne Scottlin

Dedication

This book is dedicated to *you*,
for your courage to find joy in living
your best version of yourself.

Scottlin Books

Contents

Preface

ﬁ

A JOYFUL LIFE is a present, authentic life. It is living at your full potential as a whole human being. When you live from this place of fulfillment and wellbeing you begin to observe yourself from a fresh perspective. You also become more attune to the beautiful nuances of the world around you and the impact you have in it.

Like most people, however, you may often find that your reservoir of joy is running low or in extreme cases, it may even seem to run dry. But with a little self-observation, you can begin to discover which mindsets and choices drain your emotional wellness, and which ones replenish you instead. This awareness empowers you to take steps toward living a more fulfilling life.

When you live the best version of yourself, you are present and experience authentic wholeness. So while you may think you can't generate joy on demand, you can choose your thoughts, and in doing so you can reconnect to your best version of yourself in any moment.

This is where the beauty of regeneration begins. Like a starfish that replaces a lost or damaged limb with a new one, you too can begin to restore lost parts of your wellbeing by transforming your awareness and thought choices.

You have the power to revitalize your contentment and to reclaim your joy:

- When you stop your thoughts from running wild and choose to let your emotions come from a place of intention instead of a place of fear or blame, you reinvigorate your emotional health.

- Every time you pause to observe and absorb those things that are beautiful and bright in nature, art, pets, or smiles, you revitalize your sense of wellbeing.

- When you choose to think and act from an authentic place of kindness towards yourself and the world around you—a bighearted place, a place of nobility, beauty and hope—you regenerate joy.

This book is a tool to support you in this transformation and to nurture you on your quest for greater emotional intelligence and self-actualization. Use these original motivational messages and nuggets of philosophy to help inspire your practice of self-awareness, and support you in creating a mindset for living a more joyful and authentic life.

Anne Scottlin

1

Wake Up Your Potential

❧

Wake with courage,

live with gusto,

fill your life with color,

and commit your heart to peace.

ℰ

Each new morning urges you to seek beauty in the now,

and to release the past

except for the wisdom you have gleaned from it.

ॐ

Every day is an adventure

if you cast aside your attachment to outcomes and destinations

and just go for the ride.

ॐ

Wake up with a song in your heart,

kindness on your lips

and patience towards yourself in your heart.

Each day is a new panorama
of sunshine mixed with rain;
notice the smell of fresh earth,
the groves and vines,
and not the mud on your boots.

ě

Awake with the sun,

your mind washed clean by the waves of sleep,

the refuse of the past gone with the tides

—unless you go diving in to bring it back to the surface.

ॐ

Every morning brings you the opportunity
to fill your day with the sunlight of laughter,
blossoms of compassion
and the fragrance of love.

ॐ

Even on a cloudy day
you can soak up the sun in your soul.
And if there's no sun there,
then imagine it until it warms your heart.

Look to what is right and beautiful
to comfort your heart
and strengthen your hands
to spread healing and peace.

꙲

Each new morning holds the mystery of the day to come;
each evening reveals the comedy of human plans.

2

Set Your Navigation

&

The destination stays the same,
it is your perspective of the journey
that makes all the difference.

&

Navigate the labyrinth of life

with a quiet inner compass,

a sense of purpose

and find joy in the adventure.

Slow down—the journey is often
more magical than the destination.

ੴ

You must find your own path
knowing others may not join you,
for everyone sees paths differently.

If life's course was always straight
you'd miss the twists and turns
that make it worth the expedition.

Every journey has its own paths,

every path has its own bends,

every bend is a reminder

that this moment is only temporary.

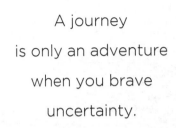

A journey
is only an adventure
when you brave
uncertainty.

———————————————

❧

Make friends with the stepping stones along your path,

for they are the building blocks that will comprise your destination.

———————————————

ॐ

Really living is to embrace the curves

life places before you,

to use the momentum

to keep you balanced,

and to enjoy the scenery along the way.

When you realize that the journey is really your destination,
you will finally begin to discover and embrace your true purpose.

_____

ẽ

Life's journey is inevitable . . .

might as well make it a beautiful adventure!

_____

3

Be a
World
Citizen

ॐ

Everyone can use a friend,

and giving your friendship is at least as rewarding

as getting friendship

so it's win-win no matter how you perch on it.

_____

ে

To seek to walk in another's shoes
is the true test of any opinion,
and the definition of love.

_____

In all places with all people,

art, nature and beauty

speak a language

that crosses all divides

— our common birthright.

If your horizon feels heavy and gray,
start helping your fellow travelers and watch
rays of sun start breaking though.

In sharing we receive.

🍎

A tranquil mind reflects a heart
that loves others and self unconditionally
and knows that this alone is enough.

———————————

ễ

Use your misfortunes to cultivate compassion;

for the broken vessel may give more freely and with less judgment.

———————————

ANNE SCOTTLIN

We are all different,

yet all the same . . .

and when we make peace with each other

we create a thing of beauty.

4

Challenge Yourself

If you want to soar with eagles,
you have to be willing to learn to fly in the first place.

ĕ

Sometimes you fear the light at the end of the tunnel

because you have grown so used to the tunnel.

❦

Wishing is desire without effort.
Trying is the desire to make an effort
when it's not too inconvenient.
Dedication is consistent effort
and the willingness to start over.

Metamorphosis is not reinvention,
it is the realization that
you've always had what it takes.

ĕ

When you feel at your most vulnerable or discouraged,

recognize it as a signal

—a call to defy the odds,

to be exceptional,

to rouse your own courage

and in so doing to inspire and lead.

——————————————

ॐ

Don't let your motivation to stay comfortable
keep you from going out on a limb
in the real pursuit of your vision.

——————————————

To stay on track
you have to actually start the train.

_____

ě

When you stretch out of your comfort zone

you take a risk, but risk is the bridge

to adventure in undiscovered territory.

_____

Notice that the wave you've been resisting
may be the one sent to carry you to new shores.

ಆ

Building courage is like building an edifice,

it grows by simply bringing one manageable block at a time.

To create the new and the daring
you must relinquish the sensible.

❧

Sometimes it's not the strongest tree that survives the storm
but the most adaptable.

The future is never certain,
but if you let fear be your master
you will never have the courage to spread your wings.

The game of life is best played
with a sense of humor.

5

Contemplate
Nature

Nature's galleries are hung

with effortless art.

Sometimes the colors of nature

are all the heart needs

to catch its breath and get its balance.

Nature's textures, light and colors
elude even the master's brush.

With each small beating heart
we share life in common,
we share a thing of beauty.

Nature is a master jeweler.

ẽ

The power and brilliance of nature

speak to something truly

ancient in us.

Nature's art puts to rest
all other claims to fame.

Just a few moments of stillness in nature

can recalibrate the mind.

Nature paints with the
finest palettes.

The power of solitude
renews us to serve the crowds
with peace and patience.

Nature's art

exceeds

the imagination.

117

ANNE SCOTTLIN

6

Connect to Your Creative Force

ಹ

The power of Imagination:

If you can think it, you've created it.

When you've created it

you can give it as a gift.

You are a magician.

ඉ

In nature, art, and music
the creative heart finds itself at home.

Imagination is just reinventing the ordinary

to create the extraordinary.

ॐ

The true artist does not care what others think
but seeks only to tap into his deepest symphony of imagination.

The instrument of imagination
must be played to stay in tune.

The idea of creating a thing
was first, itself, the creation of an idea.

There is always
a new story
waiting in the
endless worlds
of your
imagination.

7

Expand
Your
Perspective

What we perceive as reality
is often merely a projection
of our own expectations.

The window of the mind

works best when open.

_ℰ_

The need to be 'right'
causes many to sacrifice
a lifetime of happiness.

❧

We believe our perspectives are truths,

yet they are merely reflections

of our own interpretations.

ॐ

Sometimes the path you think you see ahead

is really the path you have just left behind...

open your perspective to new possibilities.

ॐ

Cost-Benefit Analysis:
Contrary to our frequent attachment
to grudges or being right,
letting go often requires
much less energy than holding on.

You can see
so much more
when you get out
of your own way.

———————————————————

ẽ

Often we already have what we think we want,

we just need to look more closely.

———————————————————

ॐ

We must examine mechanisms within us

that once served a purpose

but may now hold us back.

In the kingdom of the mind,

belief and reality

shift in tandem.

❧

Where you think you are right now
is limited only by your own perspective.

8

Relax
and
Take Your
Time

When you are present in the moment
the future manages without you.

Every stage of life brings us new eyes
to see old things differently.

ĕ

Under the canopy of time and space

we are astonished by the minuteness of our existence

and realize the futility

of taking ourselves so seriously.

ೆ

We share this moment in common

with every living thing,

and in this moment

we can choose compassion.

Climb the steps of life

with a sense of confidence and exploration . . .

the unknown will merely become the present

in any case.

Contentment is the art of finding joy in the moment,
regardless of how much you have or what you accomplish.

ই

In every age we find that the winds of change

are best weathered with our roots drilled deep,

our heads held high,

and our outlook fixed

with love upon every new dawn.

ē

Optimism is the ability to occupy the present
with equanimity and aplomb,
a practical strategy since our future
will soon become our present.

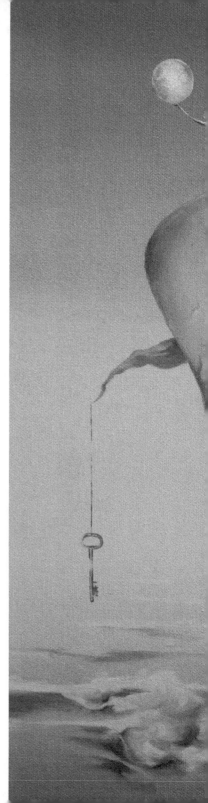

Now is the time
for open hearts and open minds
to open up the world.

9

Listen
to Your
Inner Genius

❧

All other treasures pale

in light of wisdom's gold.

_____

ॐ

Peace is not the absence of all stress,

peace is the wisdom

to just notice what is

instead of resisting what is.

_____

Without expectations
there is no disappointment.

ĉ

If you wish to make room for wisdom,
you may first need to declutter the shelves of the mind.

———————————

ॐ

Your roots may feed you and help you grow,

but left unchecked they can also hold you back.

———————————

ॐ

Break through your old barriers of habit

— it is never too late to open the windows of the mind.

An overinflated ego
should remember
that the smaller bubbles
usually last longer.

_____

ẽ

The door to wisdom
is often locked by the bolt of ego.

_____

ಌ

In all decisions fear and wisdom
must find the perfect balance.

The pursuit of knowledge is merely
one stroke in the pursuit of wisdom.

Letting go of the need to understand
is the greatest freedom of all.

10

Encourage
Yourself

Every new
chapter we
encounter
is essential
to the story,
sunshine or
rain, in the
album of
our lives.

—————————————————————

❧

Amid the jagged rocks and cloudy days of life,
extraordinary beauty can still be found.

—————————————————————

You're enough.

One bird does not compare itself to another.

It does what it was built to do...

just be itself.

ě

From the coldest of life's landscapes

stars are born,

and in the frost and snow

constellations of beauty

await those who seek.

ॐ

Pain — that undesired companion,

that indisputable evidence of living

— gives us an opportunity to practice patience in its company

and to live with greater gratitude in its absence.

ẽ

You can't stop the rain,
but you may look for things of wonder
amid the deluge and perhaps find
that even the rain is beautiful.

When feeling isolated
you can blame the world
or—you can invite others
to grab a seat and make some friends.

———————————————

ꙮ

You are never alone
— for love, sorrow and joy flow
from the waterfall of each heart
to merge with the river of all humanity,
and from thence into that sea of all that is.

———————————————

Sometimes it is during a 'winter' of life
that we pause long enough to grasp
the simple beauty of what matters most.

❦

The seagull rides on the wind of the storm
with the calm assurance that
all storms pass.

ॐ

Unless you give yourself permission
to allow joy into your life
in the present,
you are just moving away
from pain towards pain.

226

Freeing your emotional focus

from a cycle of negative thoughts

can feel impossible;

but you can begin to break the spell

by giving yourself permission not to dwell

on those thoughts

for even just five minutes at a time,

or an hour, or a day.

ě

Even in a winter of the soul

great beauty may be found

and within every frozen crystal lies

preserved in readiness

the life-infusing elixir of the coming spring.

The winds of life–forever variable–

are best weathered with the expectation that

rains will come,

the sun will return

and without both we would never grow.

There is plenty of space in the universe
to disperse my stash of troubles,
and not enough room in my heart
to make them worth dwelling on.

11

Open
Your Heart
to Joy

❧

Being serious
never made anyone
happy.

Without play,
imagination is soon replaced
by practicality.

—————————————

ě

'Choosing to be happy' may sound ridiculous,
but relaxing your death grip on your right to be unhappy
may get you closer than you think.

—————————————

ẽ

You choose what color to paint your sky,

and while you're at it

you can brighten someone else's.

The joy of adventure,

the magic of discovering

for the first time,

the beautiful and the bright...

this childhood heart is still within,

just waiting

to be discovered again.

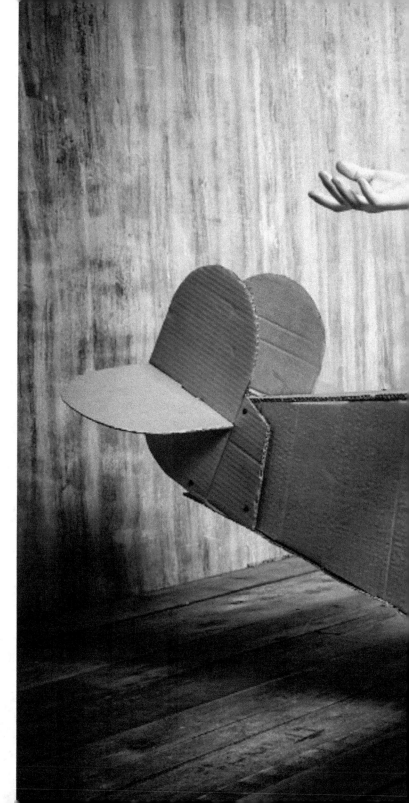

If just for one day you chose not to make

any negative judgments about yourself,

you might find that happiness is already yours.

_____

❧

You can choose to use your voice
to make the world a more beautiful place
(and you don't even have to sing).

_____

ॐ

Sow the terraces of the mind
with seeds of peace,
water with gratitude,
and nurture with
the warmth of love.

ॐ

Gratitude is the fragrance
that lingers in the heart
even when flowers are out of sight.

———————————————

ॐ

Live gently with yourself and others,

pursue joy over meaning,

love over creed,

generosity over being right;

and happiness will have already found you.

———————————————

12

Learn to Love the Endings

❦

What seems like the end
may just be the leaves of change
before a new beginning.

ॐ

Why persist in chasing
a sun that has set?
For sooner or later,
when you turn around,
you will see a new dawn
has already risen behind you.

Sunset, sunrise
— the end is just a beautiful beginning
in the circle of "time".

Mastering the art of graceful endings
is a beautiful thing to behold.

At day's end
much has been accomplished
if you have simply made
a little peace with yourself.

ॐ

Gratitude and joy

are ageless,

even as time goes by.

At the end of the day, ask...

Did I laugh?

Did I love?

Did I give?...

and determine to do that

again tomorrow.

In every autumn is the seed of spring,

in every sunset is another's dawn,

in every trail's end is a new adventure.

About the Author

Anne Scottlin, MA, CPC

ANNE SCOTTLIN is an author, consultant and specialist in emotional well-being. She leads innovative corporate training on work-life integration and individual fulfillment. A podcaster and influencer, Scottlin's popular Twitter feed draws millions of views a month and she produces a compelling weekly show. Her energy and enthusiasm attract clients worldwide to her workshops, retreats and her flagship program, The Power of Joy Transformation.

A uniquely gifted teacher, Anne's singularity springs from the blend of her academic background, entrepreneurial experience, and unusual upbringing. She also draws from her personal quest for joy, self-actualization and global vision. An aesthete deeply inspired by nature, mindfulness and excellence, Anne's approach is one of compassion, honesty and high standards.

Anne lives in Santa Monica, California, with her husband and two Mini Schnauzers. When she's not working with her clients or writing a new book she enjoys wilderness hiking, world travel, and recharging outdoors in her favorite hammock. One of her best kept secrets is that she is a Medieval history hobbyist with a special interest in medieval women writers.

www.AnneScottlin.com
Twitter: @AnneScottlin

Open More Doors
to the Power of Joy
in Your Life

Join Anne Scottlin's
The Power of Joy™ Transformation

Anne Scottlin's revolutionary multi-week experience guides you through a process to discover a transformation of joy in your life. In her innovative program, Anne teaches you effective techniques to connect to your JOY to help you reduce stress and find more success and wellbeing into your daily experience. Get access to Anne's members-only Power of Joy™ community where you can get support, have fun and grow friendships! SIGN UP NOW: www.annescottlin.com/services

The Joy in Your Job Experience!
The Business of Joy™
Corporate Training, Workshops and Retreats

Anne leads innovative corporate training for optimal work-life integration and individual fulfillment. In these participation-driven experiences, teams and individuals work together to find how joy can transform every aspect of their business performance, their professional relationships and their lives.

FOR A FREE CONSULTION:
www.annescottlin.com/services

Keynote
Motivational Speaker

If you are interested in booking Anne Scottlin to speak to your organization about use the Power of Joy™ please contact on www.annescottlin.com/services

CPSIA information can be obtained
at www.ICGtesting.com
Printed in the USA
LVHW061455241021
701370LV00008B/447